MATCHSTICK
PUZZLES

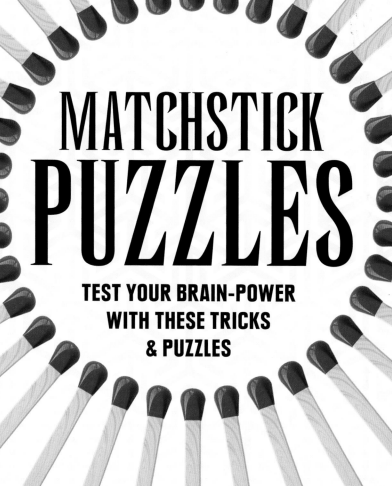

MATCHSTICK PUZZLES

TEST YOUR BRAIN-POWER WITH THESE TRICKS & PUZZLES

ARCTURUS

ARCTURUS

This edition published in 2015 by Arcturus Publishing Limited
26/27 Bickels Yard, 151–153 Bermondsey Street,
London SE1 3HA

ISBN: 978-1-84837-764-6
AD001674UK

Printed in China

Contents

Introduction

Matchstick puzzles have a timeless appeal: indeed they may well have preceded the invention of the matchstick itself!

In this book, the puzzles are arranged in three levels of difficulty, so start with the easier puzzles at the beginning of the book, and work towards the harder puzzles at the back.

Unless instructed otherwise, no breaking or bending of matchsticks is allowed in any puzzle, you merely need to add, take away or rearrange the matchsticks in order to get to a correct answer.

Many of these puzzles may have more than one possible solution, including reflections and rotations of those given at the back of this book; space does not permit us to show more than one solution to each of the puzzles, but at least if you get stuck, you will be able to find an answer.

The tricks which follow the puzzles are interesting and fun, so try them first, before turning to the solutions section, which will explain how the trick works, so that you will be "in on the secret" whilst leaving your audience wondering.

Who knows – after completing the puzzles and tricks, you may even find yourself inventing one or two of your own!

1

Move two matchsticks to make two squares.

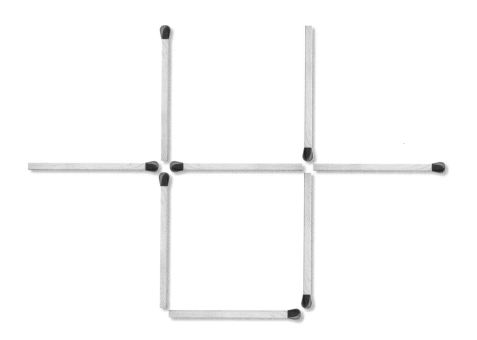

2

Move two matchsticks to turn this
L-shape upside-down.

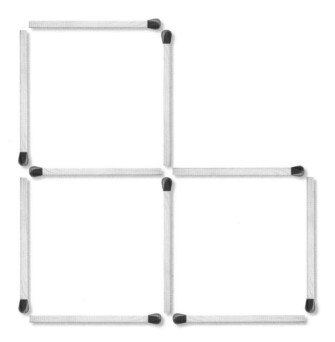

3

Remove three matchsticks to leave three squares.

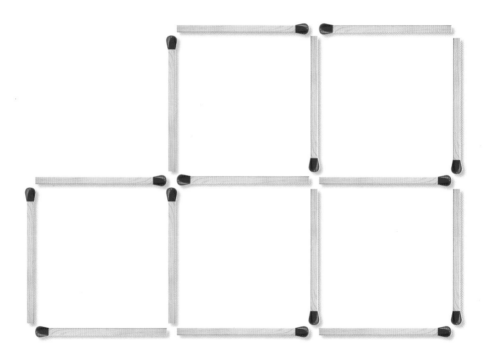

4

Remove six matchsticks to leave two squares.

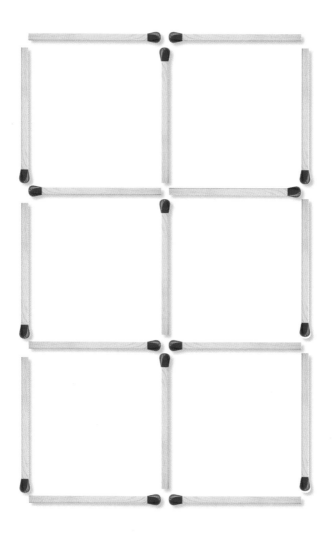

5

Remove eight matchsticks to leave two squares.

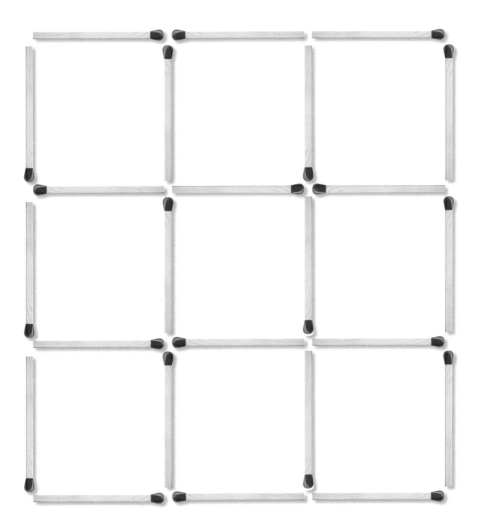

6

Remove six matchsticks to leave three squares.

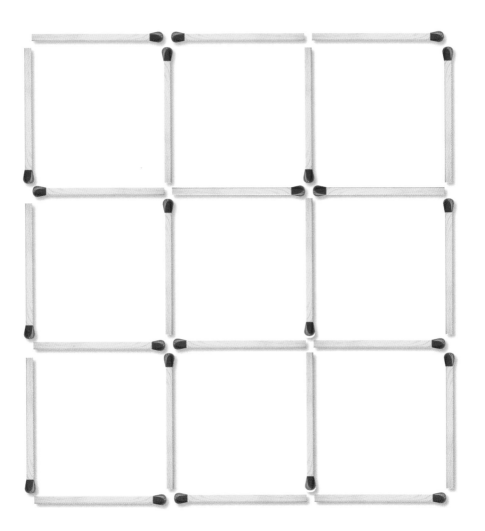

7

Here is an arrangement showing a diamond shape and a square shape. Move three matches to show a diamond, a square, and two equilateral triangles (an equilateral triangle has three angles of equal degrees and three sides of equal length).

8

Move three matchsticks to create five triangles.

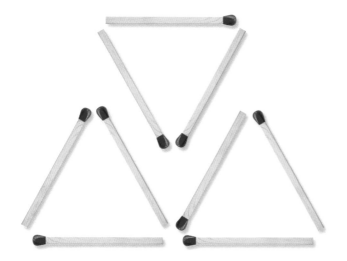

9

Move four matchsticks to make three squares.

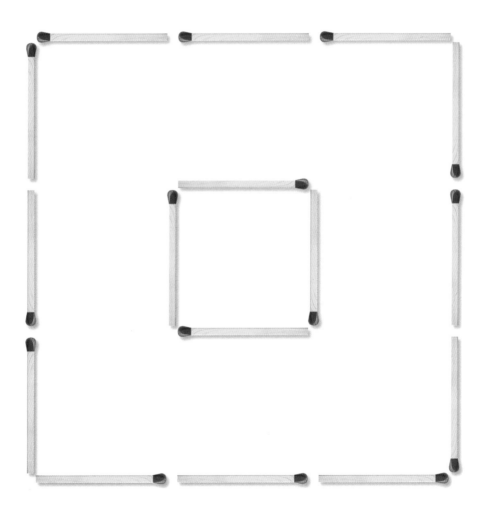

10

Here is a picture of a dog. Move two matchsticks to make him look in the other direction.

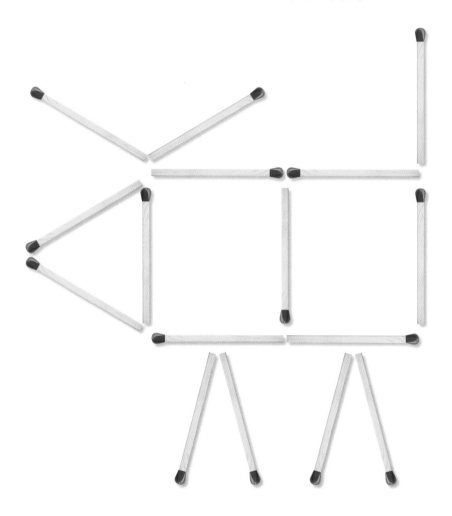

11

Move four matchsticks to make three squares.

12

Move four matchsticks to make five squares.

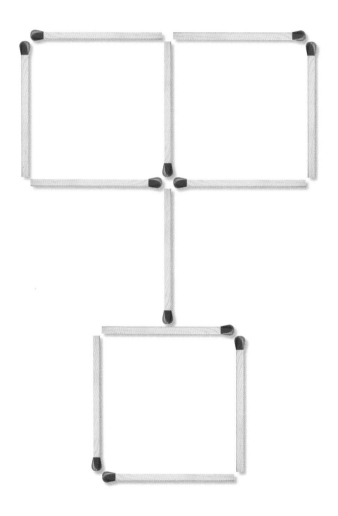

13

Remove nine matches so that no squares
with lengths of equal sides will remain.

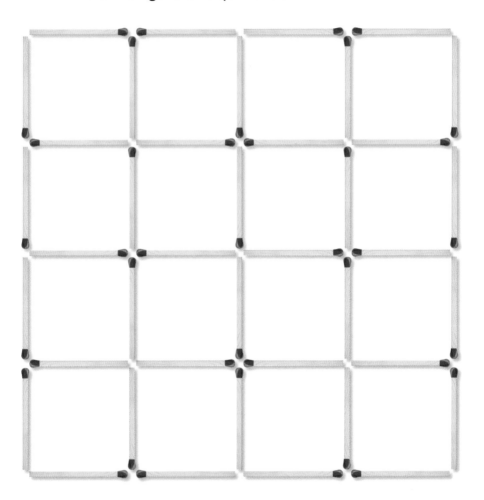

14

Use two additional matches to make a bridge from the edge of the pond to the island in the middle.

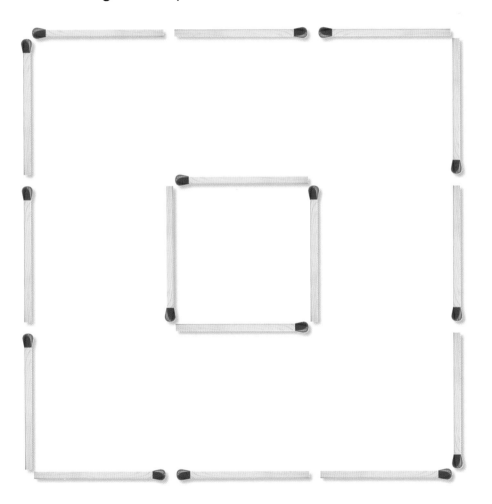

15

Divide this area into five pieces of
equal size, using 11 matchsticks.

16

Remove one matchstick to leave three squares.

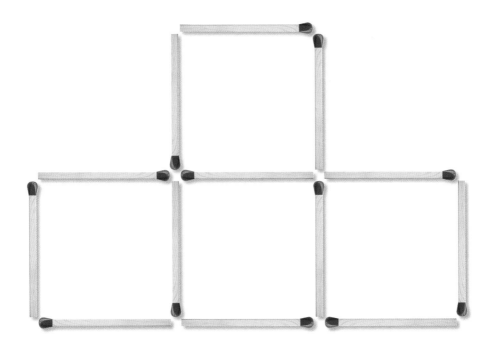

17

Here are two cocktail glasses. Move six matchsticks and change them into a house.

18

Move four matchsticks to make two squares.

19

How is it possible to remove two matchsticks and leave nine in place?

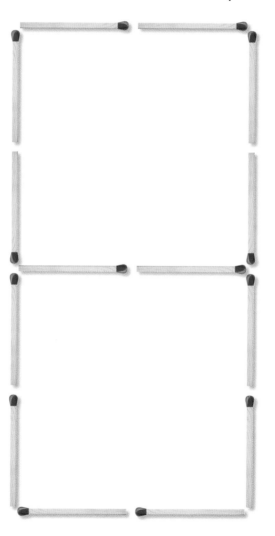

20

Move four matchsticks to make two squares.

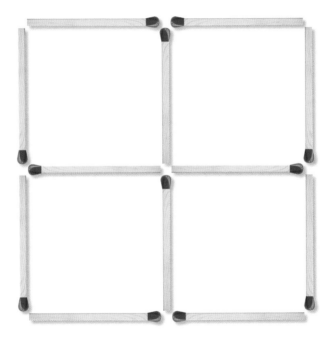

21

Here is a drawing of a house. Move two matchsticks to view the house from a different angle.

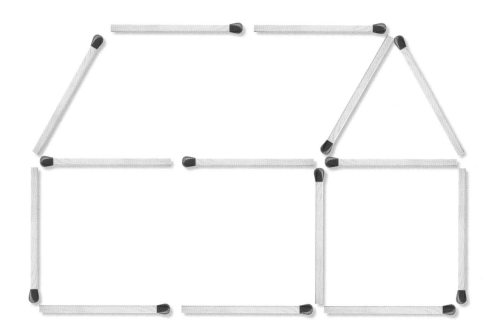

22

Remove two matchsticks to make three squares.

23

Remove two matchsticks to make this sum correct.

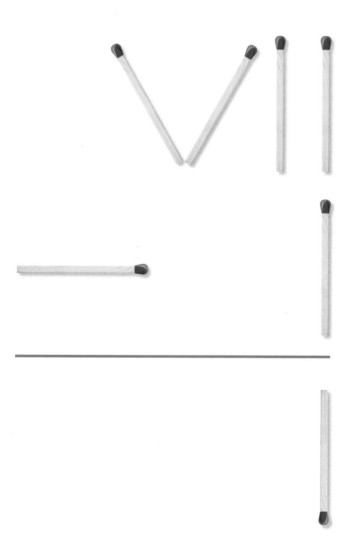

24

Move two matchsticks to make two triangles.

25

Move two matchsticks to make two squares.

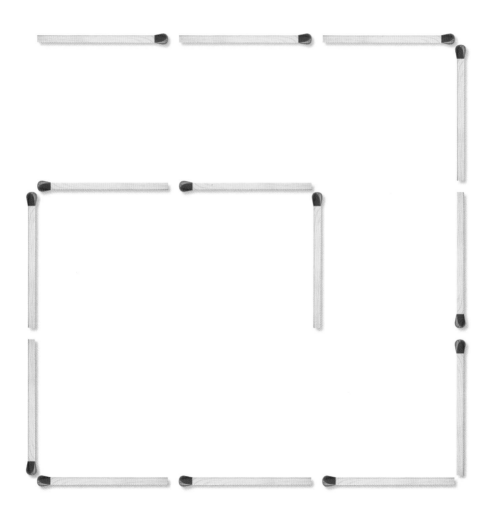

26

Move three matchsticks to form three diamond shapes, keeping within the shaded area.

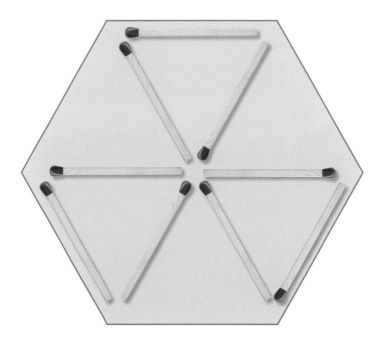

27

Move one matchstick to make this sum correct.

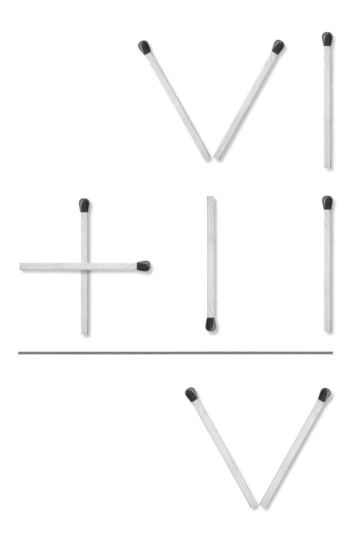

28

Using only five matchsticks, divide this area
into four parts of equal size and shape.

29

Move four matchsticks to make ten squares.

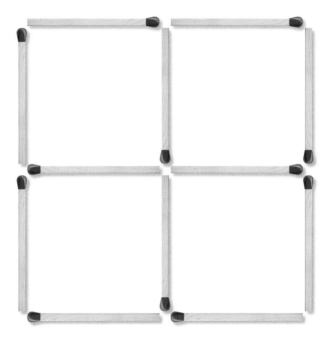

30

Remove three matchsticks to leave three triangles.

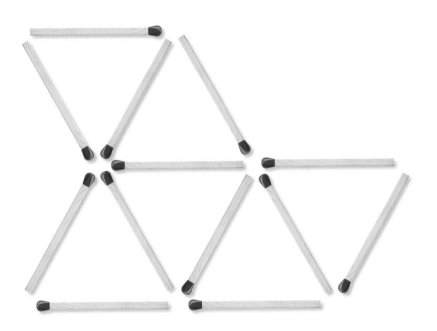

31

Move two matchsticks to make this sum correct.

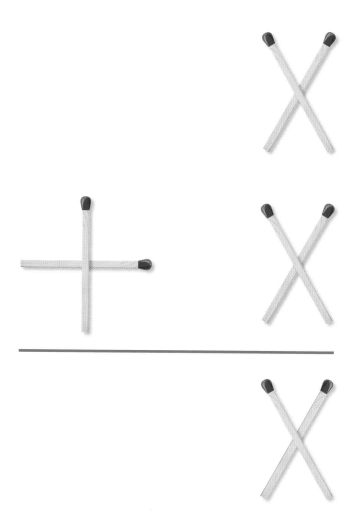

32

Remove one matchstick and rearrange those remaining to make six triangles of equal size.

33

Rearrange four matchsticks to make six triangles.

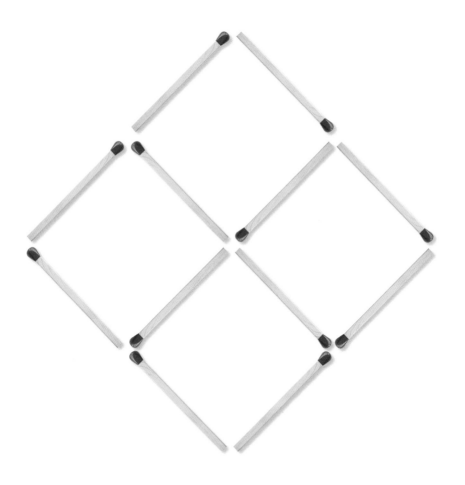

34

Move six matchsticks to make three
squares and one triangle.

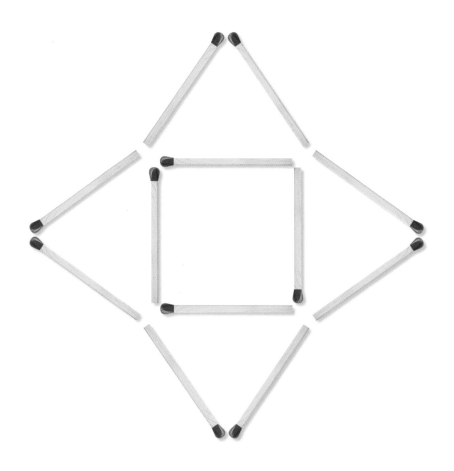

35

Move two matches to make six triangles.

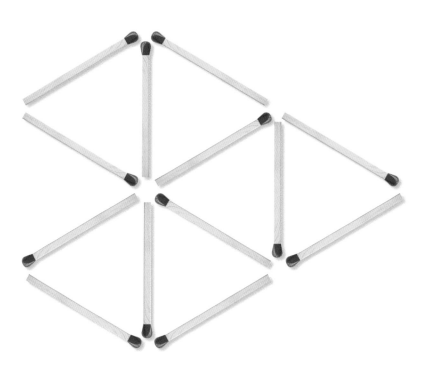

36

Remove four matchsticks to leave
four triangles of the same size.

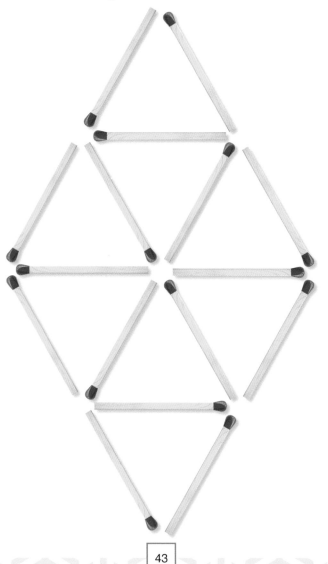

37

Move four matchsticks to make four triangles of the same size.

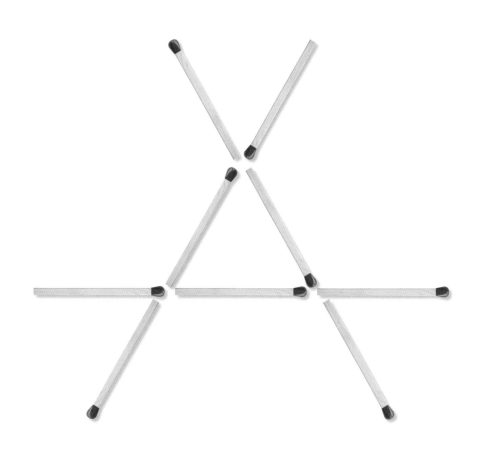

38

Move two matchsticks to make five squares of the same size.

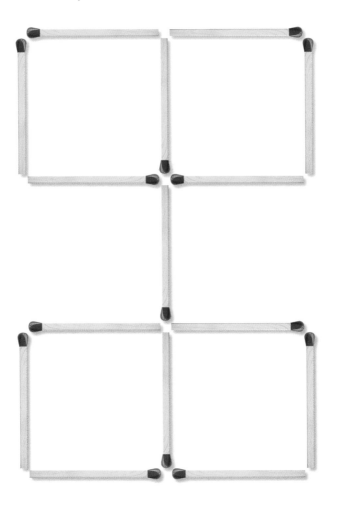

39

Move three matchsticks to make four squares.

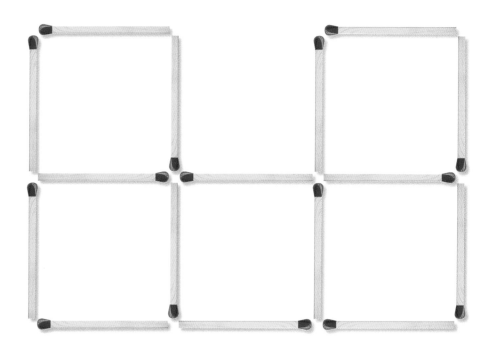

40

Which of the three alternatives (A, B or C)
is needed to fill the empty square and
thus complete the sequence below?

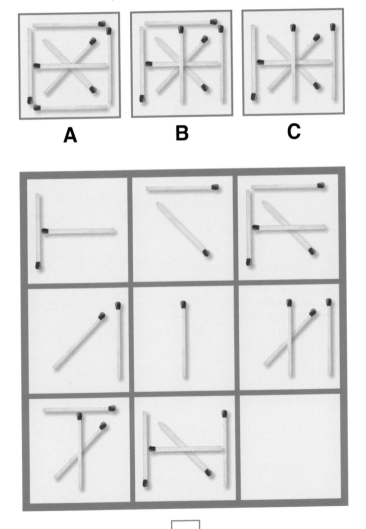

A   B   C

41

These matchsticks cover an area of three square matches. Can you move two matchsticks and add another two, yet still show an area equal to three square matches?

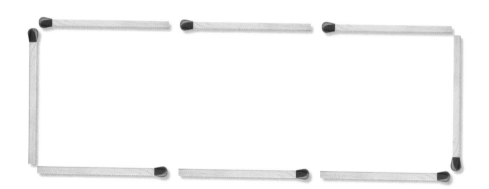

42

Move three matchsticks to make six squares.

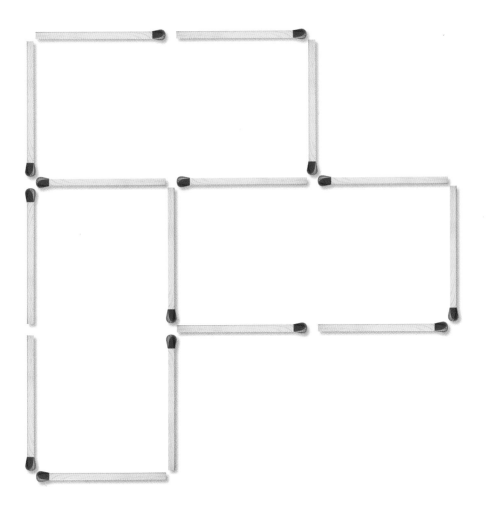

43

Move three matchsticks and the green button to
make this fish swim in the opposite direction.

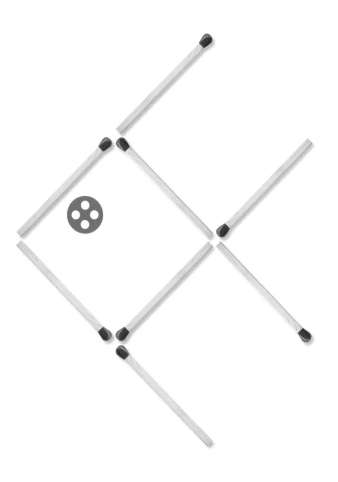

44

Here are eight triangles (six small and two large). Move two matchsticks to reduce the number of triangles to six.

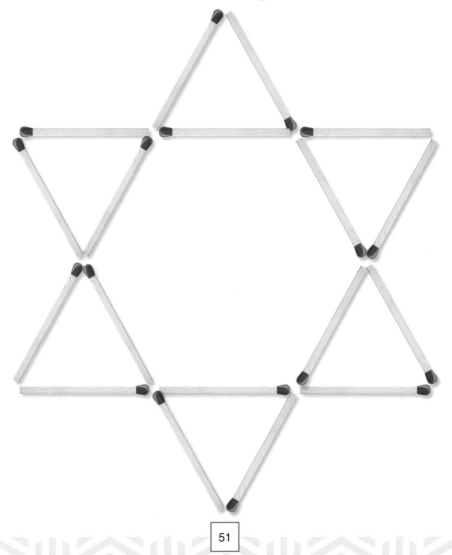

45

Remove four matchsticks (but not any
of the 12 making the outside border of
this pattern) to leave five squares.

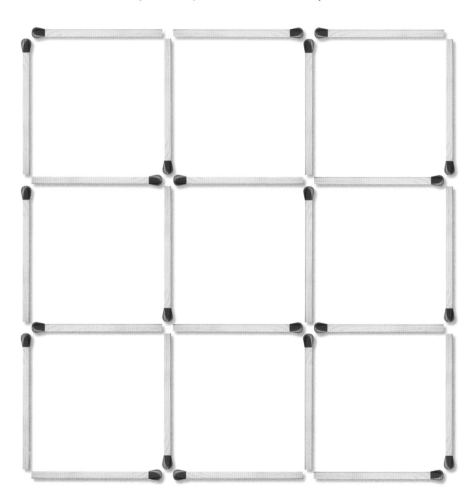

46

Remove six matchsticks (but not any of the 12 making the outside border of this pattern) to leave three squares.

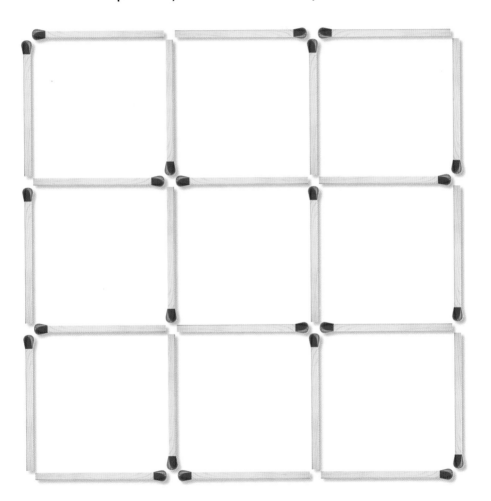

47

Move two matchsticks to make
four identical rectangles.

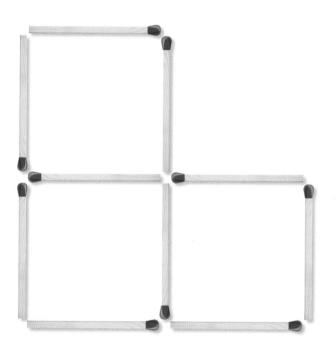

48

Move two matchsticks to make three
squares and six rectangles.

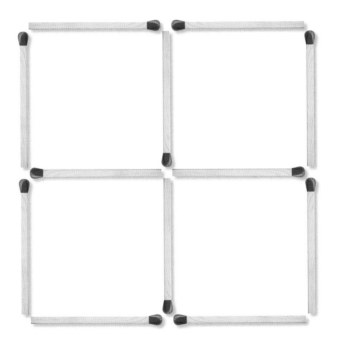

49

Is it possible to remove half the number of matchsticks seen below, yet still leave one dozen in place?

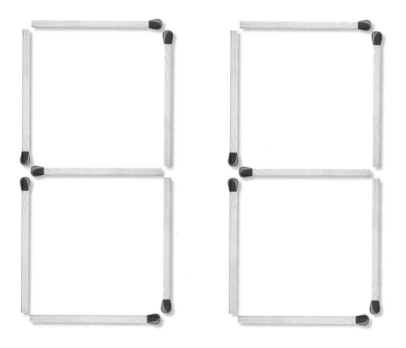

50

Is it possible to place 22 matchsticks in such a way
that each box contains at least one matchstick,
and the quantities in the three boxes on each
of the four sides of the square total nine?

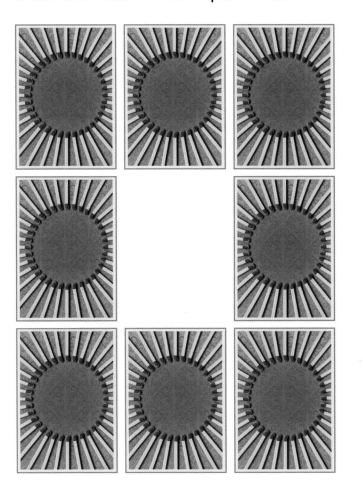

51

Move six matchsticks to make five triangles.

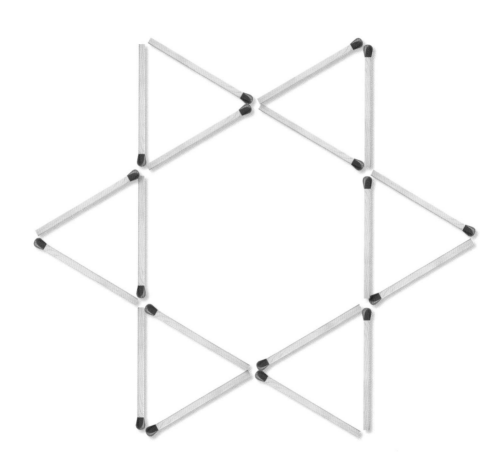

52

Move one matchstick to make this sum correct.

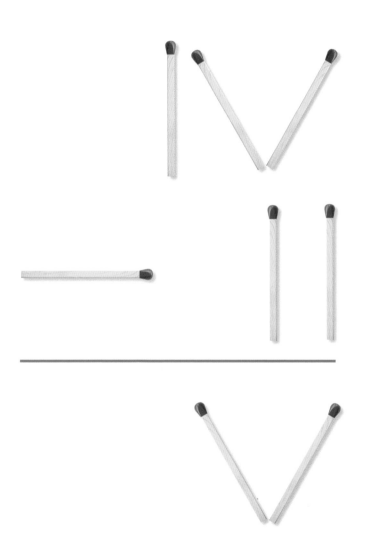

53

Arrange these six matchsticks so that
each touches the other five.

54

Remove 18 matchsticks to leave three squares.

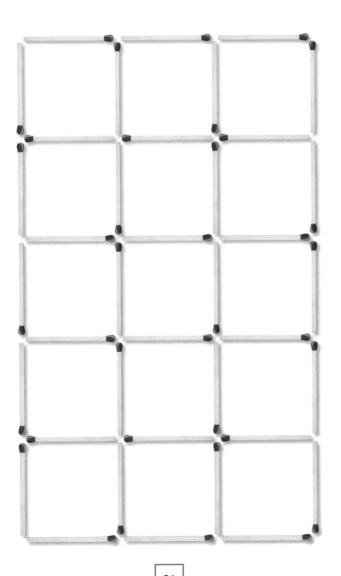

55

Move three matchsticks to make three squares.

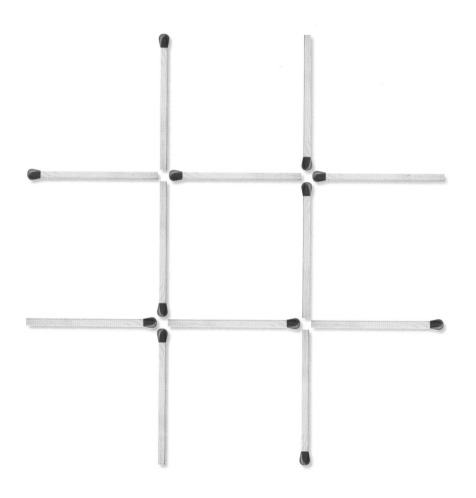

56

Move three matchsticks to make one small and three large triangles, with no matchstick overlapping any other.

57

Move four matchsticks to make three squares.

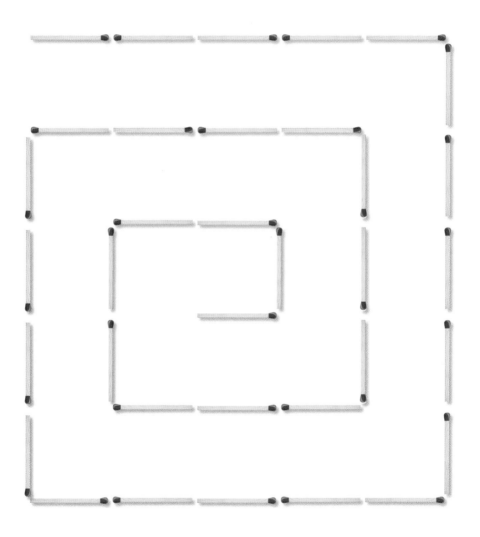

58

Move two matchsticks to show a digital
clock time of half past four.

59

In the picture below, you see four cubes.
Make one cube disappear by changing
the position of one matchstick.

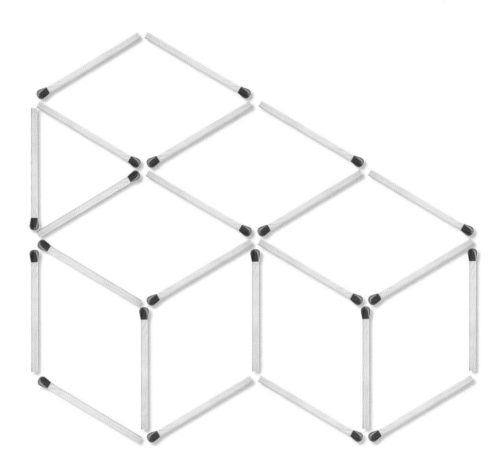

60

Add three matchsticks to form two
areas identical in shape and size.

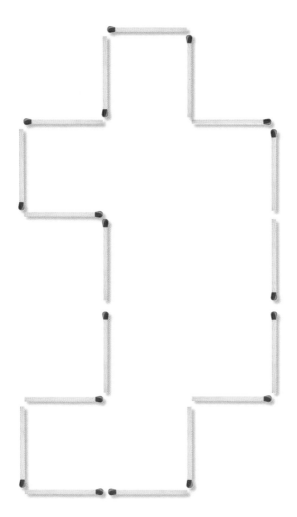

61

Using only 12 matchsticks, divide this area into four parts of equal size and shape, each containing the same number of stars.

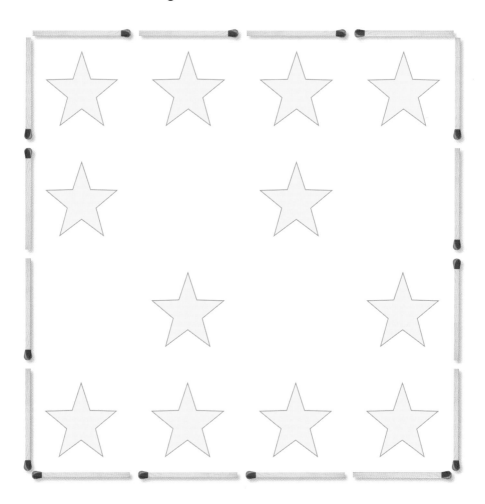

62

Rearrange these matchsticks to form seven diamonds.

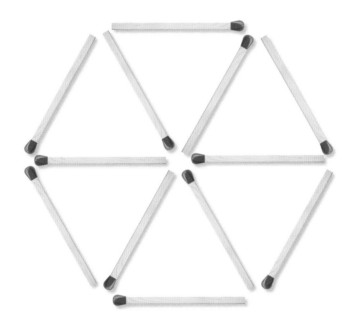

63

Move six matchsticks to make eight squares.

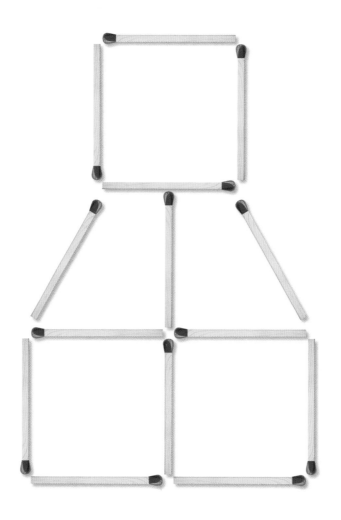

64

Move two matchsticks to make one
rhombus and one triangle.

65

Move eight matches to make six squares.

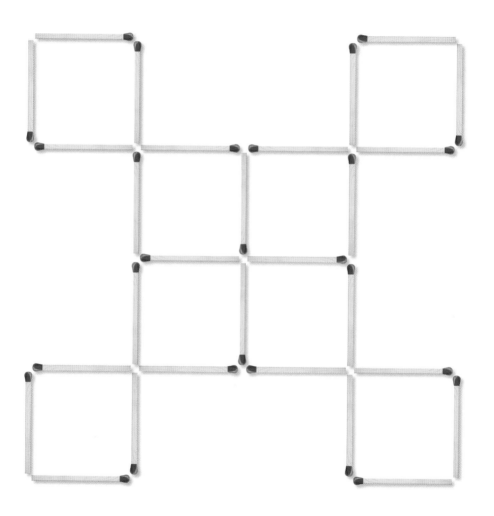

66

Move eight matches to make nine squares.

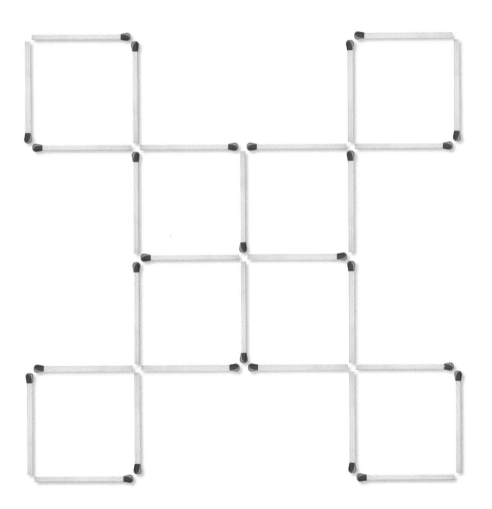

67

Using only eight matchsticks, divide this area into four parts of equal size and shape.

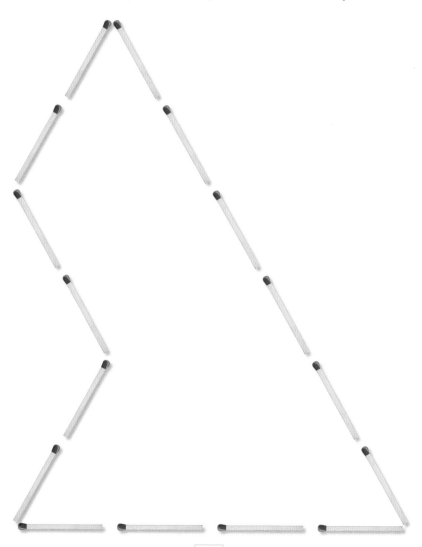

68

Move four matchsticks to make one large triangle and two small triangles.

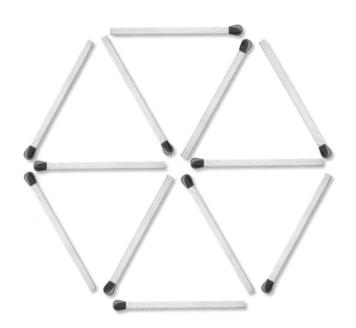

EASY MEDIUM HARD

69

Move four matchsticks to make 15 squares.

70

Use four matchsticks to divide the large square
into two parts of the same shape and size,
without overlapping or breaking any.

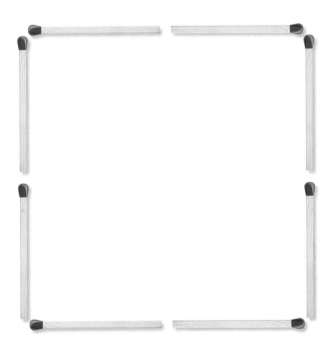

71

Divide this area into 11 pieces of equal size, using 30 matchsticks.

72

Move three matchsticks to make six
squares of the same size.

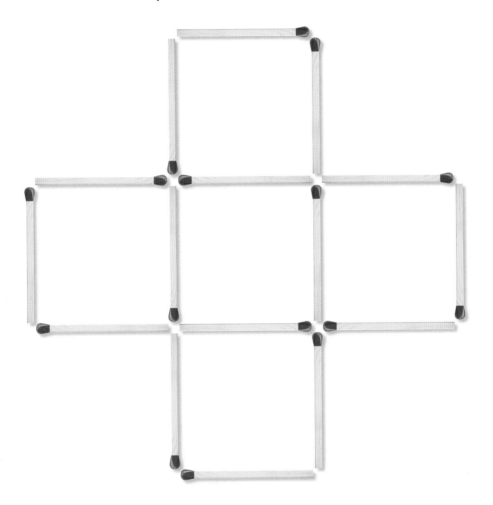

73

Remove three matchsticks and rearrange the rest to form four triangles. Matchsticks do not necessarily have to lie flat on the table.

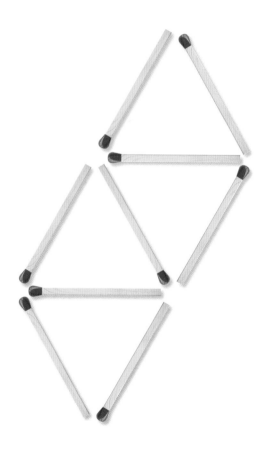

74

Rearrange these eight matchsticks to form
two squares and four identical triangles.

75

Move one matchstick to make a square.

76

Remove four matches to make nine diamonds.

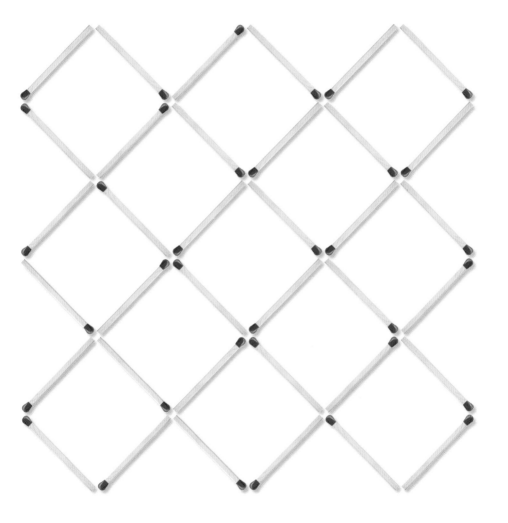

77

A farmer wishes to divide his land between his five sons, in blocks of the same shape and size. Remove some of the matchsticks to show how this can be done, whilst at the same time leaving the farm (shown by the yellow square) in an area of its own.

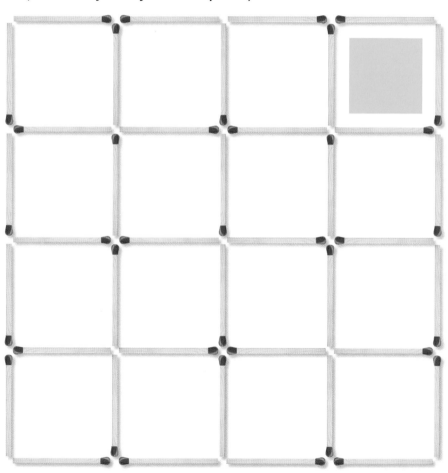

78

Here are nine equilateral triangles (an equilateral triangle has three angles of equal degrees and three sides of equal length). Move three matchsticks to make ten equilateral triangles, all of the same size as each other.

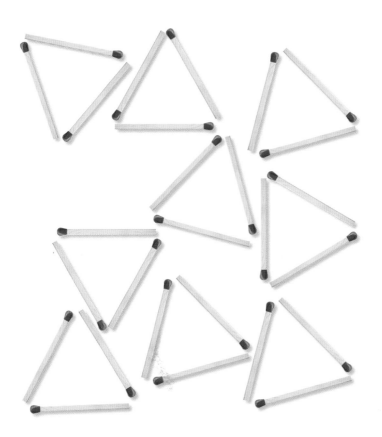

79

Move four matchsticks to create
four identical rhomboids.

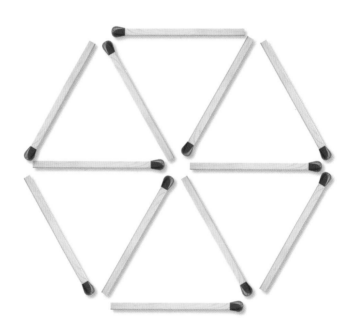

80

Using just the four matchsticks you see below, build a bridge covering the distance between these two matchboxes.

81

Move one matchstick to make the scales balance; try to think laterally for this puzzle!

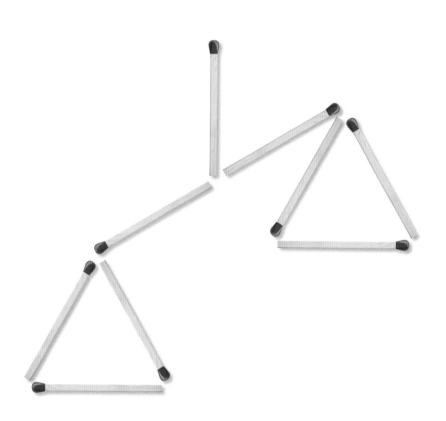

82

Rearrange these six matchsticks to form six equilateral triangles of the same size (an equilateral triangle has three angles of equal degrees and three sides of equal length).

Can you now form eight equilateral triangles? This time the triangles do not necessarily all have to be of the same size.

83

Box Clever

You will need:
· two boxes full of matches · a small coin · two rulers
· a fairly high shelf with nothing on it · and, of course, a gullible friend!

1. Take one of the matchboxes and glue a coin to the inner side of the casing of the matchbox, like this:

Manufacturer's
label

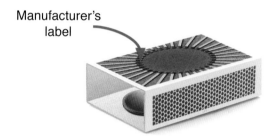

2. Now replace the sleeve and refill the matchbox. Make sure that the box with the coin is clearly marked on the manufacturer's label, so that you can pick it out as your own (filling in one of the Os of the manufacturer's name by using a ballpoint pen is fairly certain to go unnoticed by your friend).

3. Line the two matchboxes at either end of the shelf and bet your friend that if you both knock the matchboxes onto the floor by flicking them gently with the ruler, yours will land label side up more often than his, as you have a 'technique'. Tell him that to make it fair, you will empty both matchboxes, so that they are lighter and have more of a chance to spin or fly as they fall. Be careful as you empty your matchbox, in case he sees that coin!

4. However, remember that as you put it back onto the shelf each time, the label must remain facing upwards in order to increase your odds of it landing the right way up.

Why does this trick work?

84

Minted

You will need:
• one empty matchbox
• a small coin

1. Stand the matchbox on its end and then push the inner sleeve upwards from the bottom, inserting the coin at the bottom, between the sleeve and the outer casing, like this, so that the coin protrudes from the bottom by the same distance as the inner sleeve protrudes from the top, like this:

2. Now take the matchbox between your thumb and forefinger, holding it upright as in the picture above, and give the inner sleeve a sharp tap at the top in order to close the matchbox.

Will the coin fall onto the floor?

How can you turn this into an amazing magic trick that will stun your friends?

85

Snappy!

You will need:
• one hand • one matchstick

Here is an interesting trick to master, then challenge your friends!

Using only your thumb and forefinger, can you break this matchstick in half? You may not cut the matchstick, nor rest it against any object.

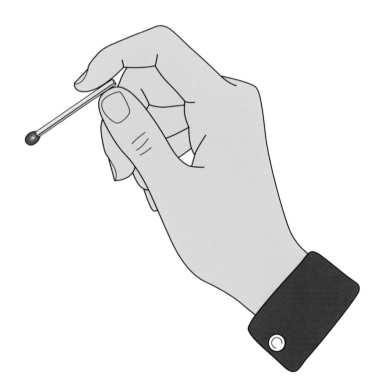

86

Matchstick Pick-Up Challenge

You will need:
• 80 matchsticks • a friend to play against

1. Lay the matchsticks in a heap on the table between yourself and your friend.

2. Tell him that you will beat him every time at this game (don't worry, you aren't idly boasting… you will win!).

3. The rules are simple: you both take turns to pick up matchsticks from the heap, and the number of matchsticks that can be picked up each time may be varied, as long as it is a single-digit quantity; either one, two, three, four, five, six, seven, eight or nine matchsticks. The winner is the person who clears the table of matchsticks.

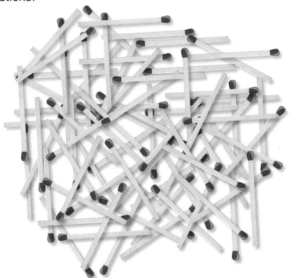

Can you figure out a strategy by which you can win every time, provided your friend always has the first turn?

87

Fair Share?

You will need:
• a pile of 38 matchsticks • two matchsticks in your hand
• three friends • a table on which to lay out the matchsticks

1. Place the pile of 38 matchsticks on a table and keep the two matchsticks in your hand, where your friends can see them.

2. Tell your friends to divide up the matchsticks (no breaking of matchsticks is allowed!) between themselves, in such a way that the tallest friend has half of them, the second tallest friend has one quarter of them, and the shortest friend has one fifth of them.

3. After a while, your friends will realize that this can't be done, at which point you put all the matchsticks back into the pile and offer to add your own two to the heap, telling them that by doing so, YOU will now be able to divide up the matchsticks between them and still keep your two matchsticks after you have finished.

4. Give the tallest friend 20 matchsticks, whilst announcing that half of 40 is 20; give the second tallest friend ten matchsticks, whilst announcing that one quarter of 40 is ten; and give the shortest friend eight matchsticks, whilst announcing that one fifth of 40 is eight. There will be two matchsticks left on the table, and you can now take these back into your hand, announcing that the total number of matchsticks they hold is 38, so you can't understand why they couldn't divide these matchsticks between themselves before!

5. Ask your friends if they know of any reason why they couldn't divide 38 matchsticks between them, before you added (then removed) the two you hold in your hand. The tallest friend (who should have received half) would have expected 19, but now has 20 matchsticks – ask him to explain why he has one more than he thought he should have received.

Can you provide the answer?

88

A Trick Up Your Sleeve

You will need:
• a shirt or jumper with tight-fitting sleeves • a loose-fitting cardigan or jacket to wear over your shirt or jumper • four matchboxes, three of which are empty and one of which is half full of matches

1. Place the three empty matchboxes in a pile on a table.

2. Place the matchbox containing the matchsticks inside the left-hand sleeve of your tight-fitting shirt or jumper, making sure that it doesn't move around.

3. With your right hand, pick up the top matchbox from the pile and shake it. Announce to your audience that since they cannot hear matches rattling inside, the matchbox must be empty; open it and show it to the audience, to prove that it is empty.

4. Again with your right hand, pick up the second matchbox from the pile and shake it. This time, announce to your audience that it is also empty (you don't need to open it and show it, because your audience is now 'trained' to believe that the matchbox is empty, since they can hear nothing).

5. Now with your left hand, pick up the third matchbox and shake it. This time, however, they will hear rattling, as the matchbox next to your left arm does contain matchsticks, and this is what they will hear rattling. At this point you can say "This is the matchbox which contains matches!"

6. Change the positions of the matchboxes on the table, in such a way that almost everyone in your audience could easily tell which matchbox they believe could contain matches.

7. Invite your audience to choose which box contains matches. When someone picks out a matchbox, open it to reveal that it is empty and ask another member of the audience to choose another box. Eventually, all three matchboxes can be shown to be empty, but take care not to let the matchbox up your sleeve start to rattle again!

89

Matchstick Triangles Game

You will need:
• either 48 matchsticks (for two players), 72 matchsticks (for three players) or 96 matchsticks (for four players) • three differently-coloured felt-tip pens or sticky labels • a table on which to play

1. There are four different colours for the matchsticks used in this game, so leave one quarter of the number without any colouring, and change the colours of the others equally, by putting a mark on them in felt-tip pen or by using a sticky label, like this, for example:

one quarter   one quarter

one quarter   one quarter

2. Divide the matchsticks between the players, so that each has an equal quantity, but do not look at the colours when counting them out.

3. Every player works separately, to make triangles, each with three sides of different colours, like this (note that no match may be placed in the position shown by the arrow, as then the triangle would not be made of three differently-coloured matchsticks):

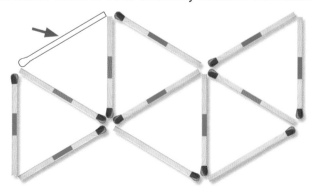

4. The person with the fewest remaining matchsticks at the end of the game is the winner.

90

Matchstick Boxes Game

You will need:
• either 56 matchsticks (for two players), 84 matchsticks (for three players) or 112 matchsticks (for four players) • a set of four matchsticks to start the game • a table on which to play

1. Lay out four matchsticks on the table, in a square arrangement, as shown below:

2. Each player takes turns to place one matchstick in a square formation, and the one who successfully completes a square of four matches gains a point. The chief thing to avoid is to provide the third side of a square, since an opponent will then be sure to add the fourth side and score a point.

3. Any matchstick placed must be at right-angles to another matchstick, like this (for example) to start the formation of an adjacent square:

4. At the end of the game, when everyone has placed all of their matchsticks, the person with the highest number of points is the winner of the game.

91

Automatic Turning

You will need:
• a matchbox containing about a dozen matches

1. Take a matchbox which contains about a dozen or so matches (any fewer than this will mean that your audience can count how many are in the box when they see it). All the heads of the matches must be facing in the same way.

2. Remove one match and place it facing in the other direction so that it rests tightly wedged between the cover and the sleeve, without being visible to your audience, like this:

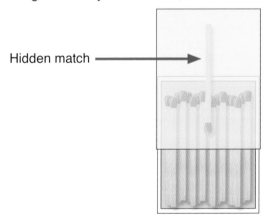

Hidden match ————————→

3. Show the partly opened matchbox to your audience, and point out that all the heads of the matches are facing in the same direction, making sure they cannot see any part of the hidden match.

4. Now close the box, pressing the hidden match into it with your finger or thumb as you do so. Give the box a gentle shake from side to side, so that the matches rattle a little.

5. When you reopen the box, your audience will see that one of the matches has a head pointing in a different direction to the others, as if it has automatically turned around. Offer the box to them, so that they can examine the contents more closely!

92

Vanishing Contents

You will need:
• a matchbox on which the label is the same on both sides: if you can't find one, use two matchboxes, carefully peeling the label off the top side of one box and sticking it onto the bottom side of the other matchbox, with the result that both sides look identical.

1. Cut the base of the sleeve inside the matchbox, using sticky tape to attach it carefully halfway between the top and bottom of the sides of the sleeve, like this:

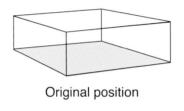

Original position

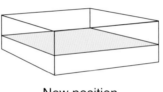

New position

2. Use clear glue to stick enough matches onto one side of the base of the sleeve to cover the depth of the sticky tape (thus hiding the tape from view) in order that no-one in your audience realizes that the matchsticks have been stuck down and cannot move.

3. When dry, place one matchstick on top and open the box in front of someone, showing them the matches inside. Remove the loose match and display it, also displaying the matches remaining in the box. Do not replace this match in the box, in case it rattles!

4. Now turn over the matchbox (making sure that no-one notices you doing so) and open it to reveal the other side of the sleeve, which will look empty.

5. Show it to your audience, and pretend to be surprised that the matches which were in the box have now all 'magically' disappeared!

Solutions

1 The matchsticks which have been moved are outlined.

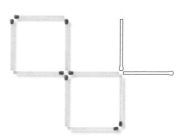

2 The matchsticks which have been moved are outlined.

3 The matchsticks which have been removed are outlined.

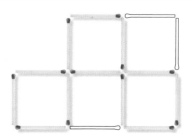

Solutions

The matchsticks which have been removed are outlined.

The matchsticks which have been removed are outlined.

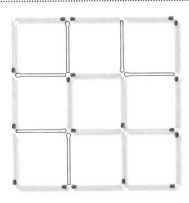

The matchsticks which have been removed are outlined. **6**

Solutions

7 The matchsticks which have been moved are outlined.

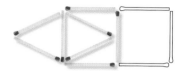

8 The matchsticks which have been moved are outlined.

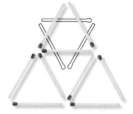

9 The matchsticks which have been moved are outlined.

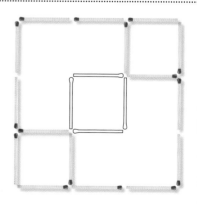

Solutions

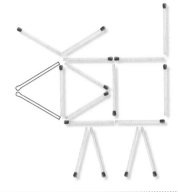

The matchsticks which have been moved are outlined.

The matchsticks which have been moved are outlined.

The matchsticks which have been moved are outlined.

Solutions

13 The matchsticks which have been removed are outlined.

14 The matchsticks have been added as shown.

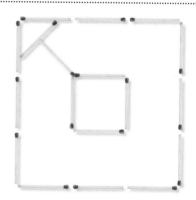

15 The matchsticks have been placed as follows:

Solutions

The matchstick which has been removed is outlined. **16**

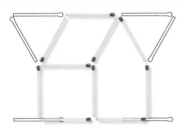

The matchsticks which have been moved are outlined. **17**

The matchsticks which have been moved are outlined. **18**

Solutions

19 The matchsticks which have been removed are outlined: those remaining form the digit '9'.

20 The matchsticks which have been moved are outlined.

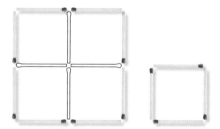

21 The matchsticks which have been moved are outlined.

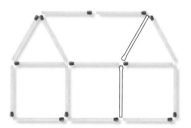

Solutions

The matchsticks which have been removed are outlined.

22

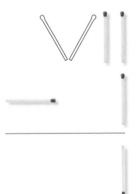

The matchsticks which have been removed are outlined.

23

The matchsticks which have been moved are outlined.

24

Solutions

25 The matchsticks which have been moved are outlined.

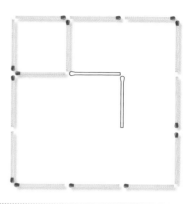

26 The matchsticks which have been moved are outlined.

27 The matchsticks which have been moved are outlined.

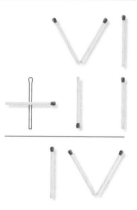

Solutions

The matchsticks have been added as shown.

The matchsticks which have been moved are outlined.

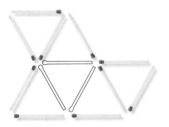

The matchsticks which have been removed are outlined.

Solutions

31 The matchsticks which have been moved are outlined.

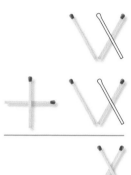

32 One matchstick was removed and the rest were rearranged to form six triangles of equal size.

33 The matchsticks which have been moved are outlined.

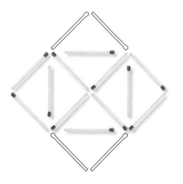

110

Solutions

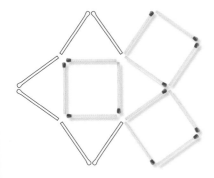

The matchsticks which have been moved are outlined.

34

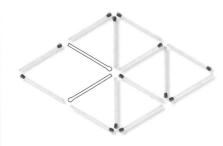

The matchsticks which have been moved are outlined.

35

The matchsticks which have been removed are outlined.

36

111

Solutions

37 The matchsticks which have been moved are outlined.

38 The matchsticks which have been moved are outlined.

39 The matchsticks which have been moved are outlined.

Solutions

B

In each row, combine/overlay the matchsticks in the far left square with those in the central square to give the arrangement in the far right square.

40

The matchsticks which have been moved and added are the ones shown slanted.

41

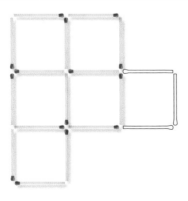

The matchsticks which have been moved are outlined.

42

Solutions

43 The matchsticks which have been moved are outlined.

44 The matchsticks which have been moved are outlined.

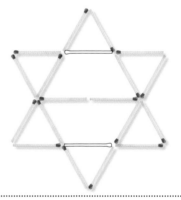

45 The matchsticks which have been removed are outlined.

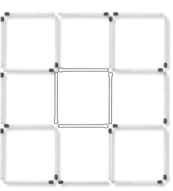

Solutions

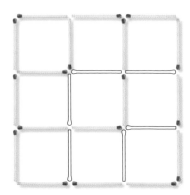

The matchsticks which have been removed are outlined.

46

The matchsticks which have been moved are outlined.

47

The matchsticks which have been moved are outlined.

48

Solutions

49 The matchsticks which have been removed are outlined. One dozen is 12, and you can leave the digits '1' and '2' drawn with matches, like this:

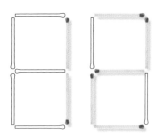

50 The matchsticks have been placed in the quantities shown.

6	2	1
2		2
1	2	6

51 The matchsticks which have been moved are outlined.

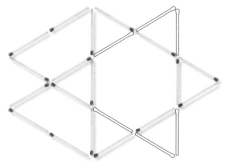

Solutions

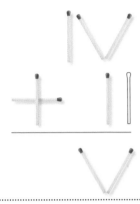

The matchstick which has been moved is outlined.

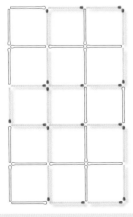

The matchsticks have been arranged as shown.

53

The matchsticks which have been removed are outlined.

54

Solutions

55 The matchsticks which have been moved are outlined.

56 The matchsticks which have been moved are outlined.

57 The matchsticks which have been moved are outlined.

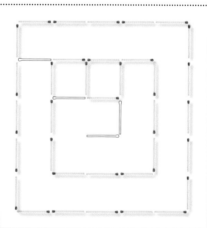

Solutions

The matchsticks which have been moved are outlined.

The matchstick which has been moved is outlined.

The matchsticks have been added as shown.

Solutions

61 The matchsticks have been added as shown.

62 The matchsticks which have been moved are outlined.

63 The matchsticks which have been moved are outlined.

Solutions

The matchsticks which have been moved are outlined.

64

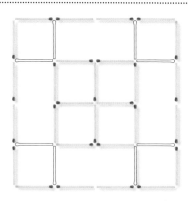

The matchsticks which have been moved are outlined.

65

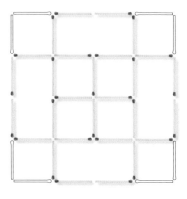

The matchsticks which have been moved are outlined.

66

Solutions

67 The matchsticks have been added as shown.

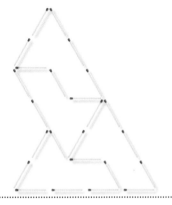

68 The matchsticks which have been moved are outlined.

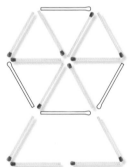

69 The matchsticks which have been moved are outlined.

Solutions

The matchsticks have been added as shown.

70

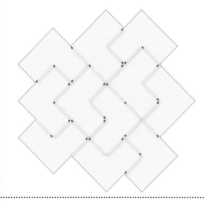

The matchsticks have been placed as follows:

71

The matchsticks which have been moved are outlined.

72

Solutions

73 Make a base of three matchsticks
and stand the remaining three
so they meet at the top, forming
a tetrahedron. The matchsticks
which have been moved or
removed are outlined.

74 The matchsticks have been
arranged as shown.

75 Slide the top matchstick up a little.
A square appears where the four
matchsticks meet in the middle.

Solutions

The matchsticks which have been removed are outlined. There are eight small diamonds and one large diamond.

76

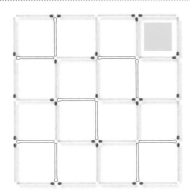

The matchsticks which have been removed are outlined.

77

The matchsticks which have been moved are outlined.

78

Solutions

79   The matchsticks which have been
moved are outlined.

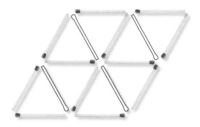

80   The matchsticks interlock, holding
the bridge together.

81   View this in perspective. The
matchstick which has been moved
is outlined.

Solutions

The same arrangement can be used twice: in the first instance, there are six small equilateral triangles; and in the second instance, there are six small equilateral triangles and you can also count the two large triangles, each made of three matchsticks.

82

The trick works because the heaviest side will turn so that it is face down on the way to the floor, leaving the label side (the lighter side) facing upward. Try as he might to copy your so-called technique, your friend will fail, since your matchbox is weighted to fall that way!

83

Instead of falling to the floor, as you might expect, the coin shoots up inside the box.

To turn this into a magic trick that will stun your audience, hide a coin in the hand you will use to hit the box, of a different value to the one you will put in the box. Show your audience the coin before placing it in the box, asking them to examine it and call out its value.

At the same time as you drop your hand to close the box, drop the coin it holds onto the floor, then ask a member of your audience to pick it up and examine it, calling out its value.

You will need to be very careful not to let the coin in the box reveal its presence by rattling!

84

Solutions

85 Curl your forefinger around the matchstick, holding it in place between the joints, so that your finger acts as a vice, then move your thumb in an upward direction, snapping the matchstick.

86 After your friend has chosen a quantity of matchsticks, you need to make sure that the number you pick up makes a total of ten when added to those he picked up. For example, if your friend takes one, you take nine; if he takes two, you take eight; if he takes three, you take seven; if he takes four, you take six; if he takes five, you take five; if he takes six, you take four; if he takes seven, you take three; if he takes eight, you take two; and if he takes nine, you take one. In this way, ten matchsticks are taken from the pile each time he and you take turns. No matter how many your friend takes from the pile at the end of the game, you will always be left with a quantity of nine or fewer to pick up, and thus win the game.

87 In everyone's rush to share out the matchsticks, it would very probably have been overlooked that the fractions (one half, one quarter, and one fifth) do not total one!
The number 38 is not divisible by four or five. The number 40 is divisible by two, four and five, in the proportions 20-10-8, which totals 38 (giving you back your original two matchsticks), but even though everyone will think that they have the correct number of matchsticks from those 40 (one half=20, one quarter=10 and one fifth=eight), the half, quarter and fifth only amount to 95% of a whole number. Thus 38 is nineteen-twentieths of 40, and the two matchsticks you hold in your hand represent one-twentieth of 40.